The Battle of the Restigouche

Judith Beattie and Bernard Pothier

Studies in Archaeology, Architecture and History

Parks Canada
Canadian Heritage

©Minister of Supply and Services Canada, 1978, 1996

Available in Canada through local bookstores or by mail from the Canada Communication Group — Publishing, Supply and Services Canada, Ottawa, Ontario, K1A 0S9.

Published under the authority
of the Minister of the Department of Canadian Heritage,
Ottawa, 1996.

Production: Suzanne H. Rochette and Suzanne Adam-Filion

Parks Canada publishes the results of its research in archaeology, architecture and history. A list is available from Publications, National Historic Sites Directorate, Parks Canada, 1600 Liverpool Court, Ottawa, Ontario, K1A 0M5.

Canadian Cataloguing in Publication Data

Beattie, Judith

The Battle of the Restigouche

(Studies in Archaeology, Architecture and History,
ISSN 0821-1027)
Previously published in: Canadian Historic Sites: Occasional
Papers in Archaeology and History. Canada. National Historic Parks and
Sites Branch, 1977.
Issued also in French under title: La bataille de la Ristigouche.
Includes bibliographical references.
ISBN 0-660-16384-5
Cat. no. R61-2/9-62E

   1. Restigouche River (N.B. and Québec), Battle of, 1760.
   I. Pothier, Bernard.
   II. Parks Canada.
   III. Title.
   IV. Series.

E199.B42 1996   971.510'1   C96-980016-9
FC384.B42 1996

Contents

Introduction 4

Background to the Fleet's Departure for New France 4

The Voyage from Bordeaux to Canada 11

Chaleur Bay 13

Reactions to the Fleet's Arrival 14

The Battle 21

Sequels to the Battle 36

Conclusion 42

Notes 44

Referenced Cited 47

Introduction

Over the past 200 years, the facts of the battle of the Restigouche have been forgotten or altered by imaginative and misinformed storytellers. The bullets, buttons and bones found on local farms, the occasional glimpse of charred timbers protruding from shallow waters, and a desire to explain such phenomena have helped to form a tragic tale parading as a description of the battle. Also, those who disdain popular legend view the battle as poorly documented. When Doughty published a collection of documents on the battle[1] it was considered to be a complete record or, if not complete, certainly sufficient for such a trivial battle.

It is as a minor engagement in the Seven Years' War that the battle of the Restigouche has most frequently been described, when described at all. But although the French fleet was small and although the battle was waged in an obscure part of the Atlantic coast, the battle's outcome was significant for the future of New France. Because the French fleet never delivered its stores to the beleaguered troops at Montréal, the troops were forced to abandon their attempt to regain Quebec City. Nor could the French establish a strong base in Acadia. Eventually Montréal itself capitulated and New France became British. These events may not have been necessary results of the battle of the Restigouche, but were precipitated by the loss of the fleet.

Background to the Fleet's Departure for New France

In the autumn of 1759 New France desperately needed France's help. Montréal was short of food and military supplies for the troops there. With the British triumphant in Quebec City and the Fortress of Louisbourg, morale was low. Only a swift and generous French response to local demands could restore confidence and make reconquest practical.

All officials in New France were concerned with the situation. Vaudreuil, the governor, repeatedly demanded French support. Bigot, the intendant, and Lévis, the head of the forces, repeated Vaudreuil's pleas, and Joseph Cadet, the *munitionnaire* (commissary) whose organizational skills were so greatly required, endorsed their appeals.

Cadet had previously been successful in organizing the supply of the colony. He lived in New France

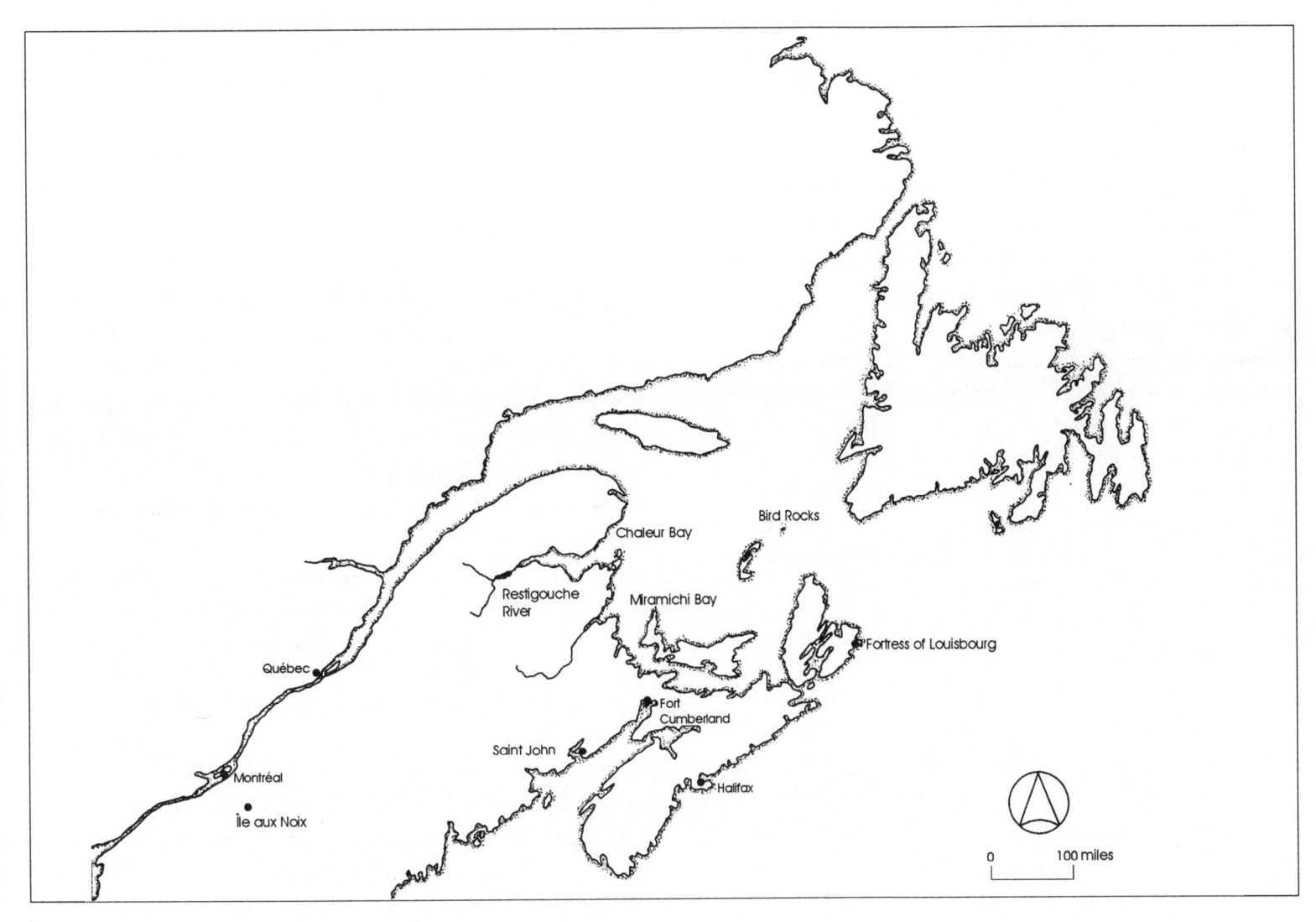

1 Location of Restigouche river. (*Map: S. Epps*)

which enabled him to personally estimate the quantity and quality of supplies required and to supervise their distribution when they arrived. Purchase of the articles in France was left to various *armateurs* (outfitters), mostly from Bordeaux, with whom he corresponded. The process was lucrative for both *munitionnaire* and *armateurs*, but apparently those who depended on the supplies were satisfied. Lévis wrote to Berryer, minister of the colonies:

I cannot forebear from giving you the best reports about Sieur Cadet, the munitionnaire général of this colony. He is most zealous for the good of the service and has had the most ample resources to supply the armies — which was possible only at enormous expense.... Unless you are good enough to show consideration for his expenses, I am convinced that the losses will be quite considerable.[1]

Cadet's skills can be judged by his previous success in an unpredictable and difficult business, but the private financiers on whom he depended were becoming unwilling to cope with the increasingly effective British navy. The only hope for the survival of New France was state aid, but officials in New France feared that their letters would not seem as urgent as the blockades and battles with which France had to contend in Europe. Therefore Vaudreuil sent with the bundles of letters a personal messenger, the Chevalier Le Mercier, head of the artillery. It was Le Mercier's mission to gain from the state the supplies that the military would require to retake Quebec City the next spring.

Le Mercier had a difficult task to perform and the recommendations he carried with him were designed to add weight to his demands. Vaudreuil declared him to be "zealous and full of integrity by reputation"[2] and Lévis testified to Le Mercier's preparation for the mission: "I instructed him in my way of thinking.... I took him with me everywhere that I had business, and no one can give you better reports than I."[3] This indoctrination program was designed to enable Le Mercier

to specify our requirements, to explain our situation to you; and regardless of what it is, I venture to assure the minister that the colony will not be taken before the month of May. This will allow time to send us the help which the King may be pleased to provide you with.[4]

On the evening of 25 November 1759 Le Mercier, with his precious bundle of letters, left Sillery aboard the *Machault* in the company of a few of the ships which had been conveyed to Quebec City in the spring of 1759. After fighting his way past the British fleet and land-batteries, Captain Kanon conducted the messenger to Brest on 23 December 1759 and personally accompanied him to Versailles.

France had not entirely forgotten New France's plight. In early December, the Committee of General Marine Service had read and approved a plan of action against the British and amongst its recommendations appeared: "it seems indispensable to send to Canada, by 15 February 1760 at the latest, assistance in the form of provisions and munitions to enable those who thus far have so bravely resisted there to hold out."[5]

This vague plan at least prepared the officials for the more detailed and more urgent demands voiced by Le Mercier. Because they express so fully the dire straits into which New France had fallen, Le Mercier's entire memorandum is quoted:

Report on the Situation in Canada, limited to what is required if this colony is to be retained by the King until Spring 1761.

Article 1
France can retain these possessions in North America only by sending assistance there in the form of men, munitions of war and provisions, under the escort of five or six men-of-war.

Article 2
The success of this enterprise will depend on the outfitting activity, which must be completed in February in order to forestall the enemy in the [St. Lawrence] River.

Article 3
It is necessary to lay siege to Quebec City and to take it in the month of May, at which time the enemy cannot round Île aux Noix because of the high spring waters.

Article 4
The purpose of the men-of-war and frigates will be not only to escort the fleet, but also to arrest the enemy squadron if it pursues us closely.

Article 5
Entrenched batteries would be set up on Île aux Coudres and the North Shore to force the English to attack them.

Article 6
The men-of-war would remain anchored in the small river so as to be able to attack enemy vessels or frigates that may have passed the Gouffre.

Article 7
If the English had reached the Gouffre with much superior naval forces, then our squadron would go

and moor broadside above the bar to stop the enemy there and would beach one or two frigates alongside St. Joachim to prevent it from sailing with frigates or transports around the north end of Île d'Orléans.

Article 8

Twenty 36-pounders can be put aboard to ballast the men-of-war. With these, batteries would be set up at Pointe de Lévis and at the southwest tip of Île d'Orléans. These would cover our vessels' retreat and prevent the English vessels from dropping anchor under the Québec cannon.

Article 9

Assuming that it were necessary in the end to yield to force, the men-of-war and frigates would proceed to drop anchor above the Sault de la Chaudière. The siege force would have set up a redoubt there, and another on the opposite shore, to receive guns and mortars. This is the narrowest part of the river.

Article 10

The number of men must be at least 4000, including both troops from Île Royale de la Colonie and volunteers from the regiments. This would mean only 8000 soldiers in Canada, both to protect the frontiers and for the siege of Quebec City, whose garrison has 4000 or 5000 men.

It will be noted that these soldiers will not be an expense. It should be less expensive to transport them because they will take the place of crew in the transport ships and will be used for work below decks.

Article 11

Not less than 50 quintaux of flour can be sent, assuming only 20,000 rations per day, of a livre and a half of bread each, although it should be two livres. Thirty-six livres of flour per month will be needed for each ration, or 7200 quintaux per month, and for the seven months of the campaign, 50,400 quintaux. It is clear that it will be necessary to harvest enough to supply 800 soldiers, the post workers and the Indians of the various nations over the winter, counting only 20,000 rations; last summer nearly 30[,000] were consumed.

Article 12

Twenty-thousand quarts of lard [salt pork], or at least 15,000, will be needed; 20,000 half-livre rations during the seven months of the campaign makes 21,000 Qx. for 10,000 rations during the five winter months, 7500 Qx., which makes 28,500 quintaux net at 200 [livres] per quart, 14,250 quarts. In distribution, there is waste of 10 percent by weight. If there were some surplus, it would be very helpful.

The King could sell the surplus before it rots to people who can no longer find fresh meat, since there are no more pigs.
Article 13
Twenty-four 24-pounders for the siege; twelve mortars and ammunition for them, as was requested in the report drawn up for M. Accaron.
Article 14
The trade goods for Indians, the canvas for encampments and other necessities, as well as the cloth for the troops' and the colonists' clothing, as in the request from Monsieur Bigot, Intendant.
Article 15
Take measures that might restore the people's confidence and give them hope for the future of the paper [money], in which their fortune consists; otherwise, there can be no assurance of finding the same zeal and determination among the Canadians.
Article 16
Since dry and liquid goods in Canada cost an excessive amount due to their scarcity, the King might supply the needs of the people through some merchants to whom His Majesty would pay a commission. With a million, He would derive more than ten [million] in bills of exchange or paper [money], and this would be a sure way to establish confidence and liquidate the government's debts.
Article 17
Establish the sum for which the Intendant will draw bills of exchange, so that they may be paid and drawn exactly in proportion to the remittance that each person would make. Order the registration of the year's bills so that they may pay income to the individual.
Article 18
If this assistance reaches Canada after the arrival of the enemy's naval forces, they [the French naval forces] would not be able to relieve the Colony [and] would be a complete loss to the King. A twofold plan might be developed which would only be unsealed in that event.
Article 19
Specific orders must be given to enter into the ice immediately upon arriving; nothing is more unusual than to see a ship sink in the ice, and it would be preferable for this misfortune to occur to one or two than to enter the river too late.
Article 20
If France does not send enough assistance to lay siege to Quebec City, it is useless to send [any] and the Colony will definitely be lost.

Article 21

If the King decides to send the assistance requested to Canada, it is thought certain that, if it arrives before the English assistance, Quebec City will be retaken; that, having nothing more to fear by the River, the whole Colony can go either to the rapids or to Île aux Noix and that the enemy will not penetrate; moreover, we have the greatest hopes for the success of the unity that prevails between M. de Vaudreuil and the Chevalier de Lévis, whose sole aim is the safety of the Colony and the glory of the King's arms.

Article 22

Depending on the course of action that His Majesty takes regarding Canada, it would be essential to send a frigate to Baye Française, twelve leagues from the mouth of the Rivière St-Jean, to put ashore Sieur St. Simon or some other officer of the Colony, to bring overland, with three Acadians, dispatches to the General in cipher.

The same frigate might then sail between Baston [Boston] and Halifax, send to somewhere in Newfoundland the captured provisions it would take, and bring them into the River as soon as the ice allows.

Article 23

Finally, we ask that you be mindful that time is passing and that only great enterprise will give hope of success.[6]

The colony's case had been laid before the court. It was in France that the fate of the expedition lay. Between the private businessmen and the state an amicable arrangement would have to be negotiated in the short time available.

In early December, the president of the Navy Board outlined the aims of the expedition to the Gradis brothers when he invited them to send their ships to New France:

It is a matter of promptly sending to Canada the assistance that circumstances may allow in order to put this colony in a position to sustain itself next year.... My intention is not to spend more than can be afforded and to prefer prompt, albeit meagre assistance, to potent assistance the preparations for which would give away its purpose and delay the expedition. I thought this course of action preferable to any other.[7]

Even though, to judge from a notation, this letter was never sent, it states succinctly the official attitude that was to cause excessive delays. One problem was to fit out the ships at the lowest price. The Desclaux price was taken as a model until the outfitters stated in late January that the lateness of the season prevented them from furnishing the promised amounts of salt beef and salt pork, and their price changed. Contracts were negotiated with several outfitters: the *Machault*, owned by Cadet, was outfitted by Ravesies and Louis Cassan; Cadet's other ship, the *Bienfaisant*, was fitted by Lamaletie; the *Soleil* and the *Fidélité* were armed by Desclaux, Bethmann and Imbert; and the *Aurore* and the *Marquis de Malauze* by Lamaletie.[8] Specific contracts were made with the Sieur Lagarosse for "vests, stockings, blankets, hammocks" and with the Sieur Lejoy for 5500 pairs of shoes while arms and Indian trade goods were supplied from the stores at Rochefort.

Once these contracts were granted and their fulfillment supervised, other problems arose. The crews of the ships which had returned from the 1759 expedition demanded payment and refused to leave again. The amount of stores had been miscalculated and quantities of wheat had to be unloaded and left in France. Four hundred men were sent when 4000 had been requested and supplies were similarly reduced. The wind was not favourable for an early departure down the river from Bordeaux. When the fleet finally left on 10 April 1760, the season was advanced and the supplies carried were insufficient. The failure of the expedition was predictable.

The Voyage from Bordeaux to Canada

Led by the *Machault*, the little fleet set out down the river from Bordeaux. The complete fleet consisted of six ships: the *Machault*, 500 tons, 150-man crew, Captain Giraudais; the *Bienfaisant*, 320 tons, Captain Jean Gramon, the *Marquis de Malauze*, 354 tons, Captain Antoine Lartigue; the *Fidélité*, 450 tons, Captain Louis Kanon le jeune; the *Soleil*, 350 tons, Captain Clemenceau; and the *Aurore*, 450 tons, Captain François Desmortier. With these six, however, were travelling "a number of others placed under my escort to clear the Capes [Cape Finisterre],"[1] and it was in escorting these ships that the tiny fleet ran into difficulty. As the president of the Navy Board wrote, "it is unfortunate that this convoy was obliged to make for the capes, which is usually the place where enemies lie in wait."[2]

On 11 April, the second day out, the fleet sighted two British ships — part of Boscawen's blockade — and the signal was given "escape if you can." Following the instructions given to Giraudais to take any precautions "to save his convoy during the crossing in the event of an unfortunate encounter,"[3] the *Machault* led the British on a ten and a half hour chase away from the fleet. Night saved the *Machault*, but only the *Marquis de Malauze* and the *Bienfaisant* rejoined the frigate, the former on 12 April, the latter on 17 April.

Two ships, the *Soleil* and the *Aurore*, from the already small fleet had been lost to the Canadian cause while just off Europe. A newspaper account of the ships taken by Boscawen mentioned:

The Soleil of Bordeaux, of 360 tons, 12 guns, 45 men, laden with stores, ammunition and provision and commanded by M. Du Chambon, taken by Lieutenant Norwood in his Majesty's Ship Adventure. *She had on board one Captain, three Corporals and 60 private men, and sailed from Bordeaux the 10th of April.*[4]

The *Fidélité* suffered as final a fate as the captured ships:

On the twentieth day of our voyage, this vessel was sunk by a wave; the four officers of the troops, two soldiers, the Captain and eleven men from its crew reached one of the islands of the Azores in an open boat.[5]

After this inauspicious start in which half of the convoy was lost, the journey progressed uneventfully until the fleet approached the St. Lawrence River. In mid-May, at Île aux Oiseaux the French captured a British ship on its way to Quebec City. When they learned from their prisoners that the British fleet had preceded them up the river, they called a hasty council and decided to make for Chaleur Bay.

By 16 May the fleet had arrived at Gaspé where they encountered English ships. Duncan Campbell, the master of one of the English ships, recorded the affair:
on the 16th about two in the afternoon being close in with Gaspy I put about and stood off from it, and soon discovered three ships standing in from Eastward with English Colours flying being then very nigh them, and one of them to Windward and the other two a head. I saw no possibility of escaping them even had I known them to be french ships, which I never judged until the weathermost [the Bienfaisant] bore down and desired me to strike to the King of France, the other two bore down upon four more English Vessels that were to leeward and having got information from a French pilot that I had that Lord Colvill was got up the River. Having passed through the Bay of Chaleure they entered the River Ristigush....[6]

The other English ships captured that day were the "*Augustus*, Barnabas Velman [Captain Wellman][7] from New London, but last from Louisbourgh, Bangs

[Captain Banks][8] from New York, Cushing from Casco-Bay; Campbell [possibly Duncan Campbell], Swinney and Maxwell from Halifax, bound up river."[9] On 17 May they captured two more ships and, as a prisoner later wrote, "if the weather had not been foggy, would have taken all."[10] With their prizes in tow, the French convoy made its way into its chosen refuge, Chaleur Bay.

Chaleur Bay

Why, when faced by the fact that the British had won the race to the St. Lawrence, did the French turn to Chaleur Bay for refuge? The secret instructions under which Giraudais was operating clearly stated that in such an event the fleet was to proceed to Louisiana and St. Domingue to discharge the troops and goods.[1] For some reason, the fleet disobeyed these orders.

Chaleur Bay would appeal to the men on the three French ships for several reasons. The troops were predominantly former members of the company of Île Royale. Some had been on expeditions in the Miramichi-Chaleur Bay area about the time of the capture of the Fortress of Louisbourg[2] and knew of the posts in the area. They also knew that the British had little accurate information about this part of Acadia. But their most pressing need was food. Even though the French carried foodstuffs in their cargo, their own rations were depleted: much of the beef and horse flesh supplied for their rations was rotten,[3] the biscuit had been used and fresh bread could not be baked aboard ship. Fresh water was also needed. Of all the areas where their needs could be met, it was felt that the Restigouche River would best fulfill all requirements.

By 1760 Restigouche River was a centre for Acadian refugees. A mission for the Mi'kmaq, active since the early 1700s, formed the nucleus of the settlement at Old Mission Point. After the expulsion order in 1755, escaping Acadians made their way to the Saint John, Miramichi and Chaleur Bay areas. Macbeath dates the prominence of the Chaleur Bay area from 1758 "when Louisbourg fell and the Miramichi and St. John were raided."[4] Families began to gather from Île Saint-Jean and Gaspé when the French set up a post near Pointe à Bourdeau on the Restigouche,[5] but the difficulty of sending supplies to this area caused great suffering to the growing group of refugees. Bourdon, the head of the post, wrote in April 1760, "The scarcity is so great that, after eating the domestic animals, we were obliged to eat the skins of cattle and beavers to survive."[6] Not only did the French ships sorely need a safe, secluded harbour in which to prepare themselves for a long voyage, but the residents of the Restigouche sorely needed the stores the ships carried.

About 18 May the fleet and its train of prizes proceeded into Chaleur Bay. Near its mouth they dispatched St. Simon, the swiftest and most trustworthy of the troops, to carry news from France and from the ships overland to Montréal. The next day the troops landed on the north shore (at Pointe à la Batterie) and a camp established. While one party of sailors set to work building a battery, another unloaded one of the prize ships, the *Augustus*, to serve as a scout. Ovens were built to bake bread and fresh water was obtained.

Captain D'Angeac, now commander of all the troops, discovered the desperate straits of the Acadians at Bourdon's post.
I found in this Place of Misery more than one thousand five hundred souls exhausted from lack of food and dying of hunger who had been forced to eat beaver skins throughout the winter. I gave them a half livre of flour per day and a quarteron of beef while awaiting orders from the Marquis de Vaudreuil. This bit of aid that I am continuing to provide brought them back from death's door.[7]

Each day, as word spread of the fleet's cargo, Acadians gathered to share the food. But little was done either to protect the fleet or to relieve it of its cargo. The only precaution taken was to send out, on 12 June, a reconnaissance craft under the Sieur Lavary le Roy, a first lieutenant from the *Machault*. While waiting for the messenger to return from Vaudreuil in Montréal, the French considered themselves to be well-protected in their harbour.

Reactions to the Fleet's Arrival

While the body of the French troops were creating order in Chaleur Bay, St. Simon was carrying messages to Vaudreuil. After 25 gruelling days over the Gaspé mountains and past enemy pickets, he arrived at Montréal. With the official correspondence from France came the unhappy news that the relief mission had halted in Chaleur Bay. On 13 June, Lévis recorded in his journal: "In the night we received news from France by a courier sent from Restigouche in Acadia where our ships destined for Quebec had stopped."[1]

Other runners were supposed to follow St. Simon. On 16 June Vaudreuil wrote: "It was M. de St. Simon who brought me the first letters and I know that Messieurs Aubert and La Bruer should bring me duplicates and triplicates";[2] and on 21 June: "MM. Aubert and La Bruyère should arrive before long; they were to leave six days after M. de St. Simon, but they are not as good walkers as he is."[3] These officers arrived on 13 July 1760, a full month after St. Simon.[4]

At last the French officials in New France had received communications from their superiors. After waiting hopefully for the arrival of the fleet with supplies, they were disappointed to learn that none of the food or arms would be at their disposal. Equally unhappy was the news that bills of exchange would be discontinued. Berryer, the minister of the colonies, did express the opinion that "we shall have peace towards the middle of the Campaign," and that, "provided we can hold out against the English forces now in North America, we need fear nothing, as the enemy can not reinforce them in any way, at least not in the matter of troops."[5] A later chronicler confirmed that "This assistance, meagre though it was, might have been enough to retake Quebec City or at least to prevent the English from further extending their conquests for this year."[6] The physical and mental distress of the Montréal group was increased by the lack of enthusiasm for their cause in France, but their immediate concern was to instruct the fleet at anchor in Chaleur Bay.

Soon after St. Simon's arrival, Vaudreuil drafted instructions for D'Angeac.

Instructions to Monsieur Danjac, Chevalier de Saint Louis, Captain of Infantry:

Article 1

Monsieur Danjac shall take command in chief of all French posts and possessions in Acadia, the frontier of Canada.

Article 2

He shall set up his main post at Ristigouche in the place and position that he deems most favourable for defending it against the forces that the English might use to dislodge him.

To this end, he shall have the entrenchments and other works that he deems necessary built.

Article 3

He shall place Monsieur de Niverville or another officer of his choice at Miramichi to command the forces there that he deems necessary.

Article 4

He shall have a person of trust at the Rivière Saint Jean to replace Monsieur de Niverville, who is now in command there.

Article 5
He shall cause to be circulated in all the posts and places where the Acadians have settled or taken refuge, our proclamation of today's date and that of 5 April, and our letter concerning the battle of the 28th.

Article 6
These proclamations and the reading of the letters that we address to him under seal for Messrs. Bourdon and Niverville shall instruct him in the intrigues and ruses which gave rise to the articles of his mission, which the English unjustly attribute to the Acadians. We believe that the Acadians will have even more fully instructed him in these facts. We wish him to have the originals of the letters and other documents of which it is claimed that Abbé Manach and Abbé Maillart are the authors; he shall take every means to obtain them....

Article 7
He shall not lose an instant in determining exactly the number of men capable of bearing arms in that part of Acadia; he shall take a census of those who have their guns in working order and those who are not armed.

Article 8
He shall assemble these Acadians close to him, in whole or in part. He shall omit nothing to recall those who are at Beauséjour [Fort Cumberland].

He shall place an officer or other trusted person in all places where there are Acadians to see to their safety and shall have them execute the orders.

He shall then take a census of the number of souls of either sex, parish by parish, and of the Indian nations, village by village.

Article 9
He shall place the provisions, munitions of war, guns and, generally, everything that makes up the cargo of the frigate Machault *and other vessels in a safe place; he shall give Monsieur Bazagier, performing the duties of commissary, all the facilities that may be available to him to accelerate the unloading of these vessels.*

The commissary shall have separate inventories made of each vessel; Monsieur Dangac [sic] shall send us shipments from them.

Article 10
The storehouses and other structures needed to accommodate these provisions, etc. shall be built free of charge by the soldiers and Acadians, as well as the entrenchments and fortifications. He shall

tell them that in this we have only their safety in mind.

He may, however, if he deems it necessary, gratify with some items from the stores the soldiers and Acadians who are most zealous at work, using with care what we submit to his prudence.

No certificate shall be issued under any pretext whatsoever, the King's intention being to eliminate all expenses of this kind.

No purchase shall be made, directly or indirectly.

Article 11

The ration shall consist as follows, taking care to resort to lard only when there is no more salt beef.

Be it known

To the commander, officers, missionaries, commissary and store-keeper: one and one half livres of bread, one livre of salt beef or half a livre of lard, one quarteron of peas, one chopine of wine;

to the soldiers: one and a half livres of bread, one half livre of salt beef or a quarteron of lard, a quarteron of peas;

to the Acadians, men and women: one livre of flour; to the children: one half livre of flour.

All these rations shall be issued under the bills that Monsieur Danjac shall draw on the commissary and not on the store-keeper; he shall ensure that this ration is given only to those entitled to it and shall take the most appropriate measures to prevent any improper consumption.

Article 12

We all remark to him the secret that the provisions he has with him, particularly the lard, salt beef, wine, brandy, peas and ham, are the surest and unique resource of the colony, as are the munitions of war and small items of clothing; we therefore recommend to him the strictest economy; we do not conceal from him the fact that if, as the Minister gives us to hope, we have news of peace, or we are in less critical circumstances, we might use these items as early as this fall.

He shall exhort the Acadians to continue to busy themselves in living off their fishing, just as if they had no ration.

Article 13

He shall also assemble the Indian nations and recommend that they also live off their resources; he will assist them only in powder and shot. He may, however, provide some assistance in the form of flour to Indians close to him, it being essential to rid them of the desire to go over to the English.

He shall impress this assistance upon the Acadians and Indians and give them hope of greater as soon as peace is established.

Article 14

The provisions that were given at Médoctek [Meductic] in the winter having been kept there, he may establish a commander in that place who would advance as far as Aucpac upon news of peace.

Article 15

Monsieur Danjac's chief object will be to make war on the English who are close to the part that we assign to him; he must know their present situation and strength; on this he shall base his movements, but, in any event, he shall at all times have parties of Acadian and Indian troops of varying sizes, depending as circumstances may permit or require. He shall take advantage of any circumstances that may be favourable to him to make some serious attempts, without, however, unduly compromising the King's arms. Monsieur Bourdon and Monsieur Niverville may be very useful to him for their local knowledge.

These movements shall be continual and be made, if possible, so as to give the enemy cause for concern [and] be such as to cause a diversion of the forces that threaten the heart of the colony. Monsieur Danjac shall detach only soldiers he is sure of; it would be dangerous if they deserted him.

Article 16

Monsieur Danjac may increase the ration of the Acadians and Indians who make war. He may also give some refreshment to the sick from the provisions that will be unloaded from our ships.

Article 17

He shall avoid, in so far as possible, issuing guns to these Acadians and Indians. He shall urge them to use their own and to borrow them as they replace one another in going to war. He shall provide them only with as much as he is not able to avoid providing and shall keep an exact record.

He shall not issue any clothing to the Acadians. They can do without it during the summer and, if it is required for the winter, we shall give him our orders based on the report he shall provide us of what is most needed.

Article 18

Since we have every reason to hope for news of peace before the end of the campaign, Monsieur Danjac shall have posts in all the furthest reaches of our possessions and shall give order to the officers in command to penetrate as far as possible if they hear of the conclusion of peace and to remain there; this is of the greatest importance for establishing our possessions.

Article 19

Since the English, for their part, may seek to extend their possessions also, Monsieur Danjac shall take all means within his power to prevent them from encroaching on our lands.

Article 20

Monsieur Danjac shall urge the Acadians who have ships to come there and go privateering. To this end, we addressed to Monsieur Bourdon last winter six blank Admiralty commissions. He shall take care to distribute them to those Acadians who are best able to engage in these activities. We believe their names are Gautier and Beausoleil; we recommend them in consideration of their zeal and their services.

Article 21

We will send to Monsieur Danjac a list of the vessels that wintered at Restigouche, he shall not lose a moment in preparing the Oiseau Royal or some other vessel better suited to going to sea; he shall obtain from Sieur La Girauday, captain of the Machault, a good officer to command this vessel [and] the pilots and sailors needed to arm it, taking them equally from each of the three ships. We appoint this vessel to bring the dispatches that we shall shortly send to Monsieur Danjac for the Court; he shall see that provisions are furnished to this vessel out of the very provisions we have received from France.

Article 22

When the Machault and the other two vessels have been unloaded, they shall be free to go wherever they wish, having no order from the King in this regard. Monsieur Danjac shall only inform Sieur la Girauday that we have had warning that the English would send a large vessel to meet them, so that he may be on his guard.

Article 23

Sieur La Girauday and the captains of the other two vessels shall also be masters of the captured vessels and free to take them where they wish.

Article 24

Monsieur Danjac shall write to us as often as possible.

He shall choose his couriers and recommend that they follow such a route as to avoid the enemy.

He shall send us the inventories and censuses mentioned in this instruction.

He shall take particular care to report to us any news he may have of the enemy regarding the

prisoners or otherwise and to forward to us the papers or journals that may be found on the vessels that the Acadian corsairs shall take.
And in all other cases that we cannot anticipate, we rely on Monsieur Danjac's prudence, experience and zeal.

*Done at Montreal
June 17, 1760
Vaudreuil*[7]

Several things are evident from this lengthy and detailed document. Vaudreuil expressed little concern that the fleet would be attacked; he believed Berryer's prediction that peace would be concluded shortly. Vaudreuil also had no intention of sending the fleet on to Louisiana or St. Domingue. His aim was to provide the basis of a French claim to Acadia by maintaining posts there and to guarantee a link between himself and the minister of the colonies by the ships in the Restigouche. He decided to unload the ships "and there establish a magazine for the King."[8] There was no conflict between Vaudreuil's instructions and D'Angeac's actions at Restigouche as he waited for word from Vaudreuil. However, while a clerk, Sieur Bazagier, was travelling from Île aux Noix to organize the stores and while St. Simon, who left Montréal on 9 July, was carrying dispatches and orders to Restigouche,[9] the British were beginning to move against the French fleet.

In spite of the French precautions of sending a courier by foot and of anchoring in an almost unnavigable river with which the British were not familiar, it was not long before a British fleet was sighted in Chaleur Bay. The British had been expecting the arrival of a French fleet and their reaction was swift. Two fleets were launched almost simultaneously: one down the St. Lawrence from Quebec City and one from the Fortress of Louisbourg.

Vice-Admiral Lord Colville, commander of the English forces in North America, had been responsible for the swift reaction at Quebec City. Alarmed by "several imperfect accounts of French Fleets being in the lower River and Gulph," Colville had responded by sending Captain Wallis with a squadron, comprised of the *Prince of Orange*, the *Rochester*, the *Eurus* and three armed vessels, to search the lower reaches of the St. Lawrence River and the gulf for French ships.[10] Although he was informed of the departure of the vessels, Vaudreuil gave little credit to the intelligence, saying "I hardly think the English will send their largest vessels to attack ours which have arrived at Restigouche; nevertheless I will warn the latter so that they may be cautious."[11]

At the same time Captain Byron was leading the Louisbourg fleet to the Restigouche. Through information from the Richibucto Indians, word had been relayed to Governor Whitmore at the Fortress of Louisbourg that:

in the Mouth of the River Miramichi, 6 Armed Vessells, mounting from 10 to 12 Guns Each, and 500 men in Arms, partly Canadiens, with 5 French Officers, One lately Arrived from Old France, & four from Canada; That a few days before he was at Rastagush, at which place was lately Arrived from France Five Men of War, two of Fifty Guns, the others something smaller, with several Officers and Soldiers on board, and that there likewise were several other Armed Vessells in that Harbour, but that he could not Understand anything of their Destination.[12]

When Whitmore received this communication on 17 June 1760, he had cancelled Captain Byron's orders to convoy troops and instructed him to destroy the French force in Chaleur Bay. Byron was quick to comply.

I immediately waited upon the Governor and applied to him for Pilots for all the ships and gave Orders to their Respective Captains to get everything ready for sailing the next morning. Our sails being all on shore we got them off with the Governor's assistance before the morning, bent them, and got to sea before noon, which was as soon as the wind would permit us, having been given the Rendez vous off Point Goacha [Miguasha] in the Bay of Chaleurs.[13]

His fleet consisted of the three ships of the line: the *Fame*, 74 guns, Byron's flagship; the *Achilles*, 60 guns, Captain the Honourable Samuel Barrington; and the *Dorsetshire*, 70 guns, Captain Campbell; and two frigates: the *Scarborough*, 20 guns mounted, Captain Scot; and the *Repulse*, 32 guns, Captain John Carter Allen.

With two fleets of British ships searching for the French storeships, their discovery was inevitable.

The Battle

The Louisbourg squadron, under Byron, made contact with the French on 22 June when the *Fame* was anchored alone off Miguasha Point (most of the squadron having been dispersed by fog). Four of its boats captured an armed reconnaissance schooner which the French had previously taken as a prize.[1]

Failing instructions from Montréal, Giraudais was forced — albeit reluctantly — to initiate on his own

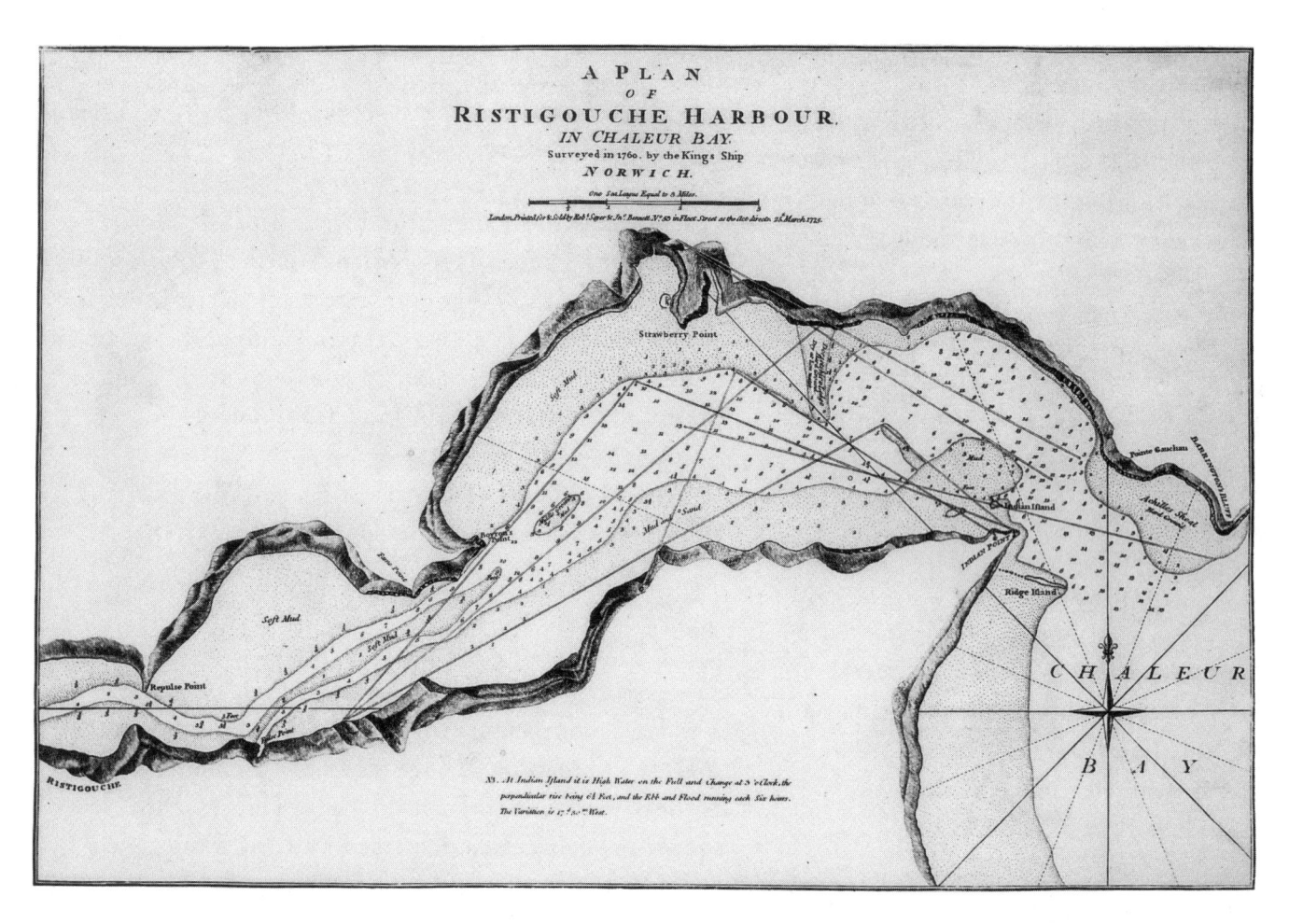

2 "A Plan of Ristigouche Harbour. In Chaleur Bay. Surveyed in 1760, by the Kings Ship *Norwich*. One Sea League Equal to 3 Miles." *(National Archives of Canada)*

the defence of a position in which he unequivocally held strategic and tactical advantages. His forces comprised the *Machault*, 28 guns (but only 14 mounted on 8 July, the day of the final engagement); the *Bienfaisant*, 16 guns mounted; the *Marquis de Malauze*, 12 guns mounted; six English ships captured in the Gulf of St. Lawrence, and 25 to 30 Acadian sloops and schooners from the Miramichi and elsewhere whose crews had joined the French when they learned of the fleet's arrival in the Restigouche. In terms of manpower, the French had 200 regular Troupes de la Marine (infantry under the authority of the Navy Department) under D'Angeac; 300 Acadians capable of bearing arms, "all capable, but lazy and independent if they are not governed,"[2] and 250 Mi'kmaq. Nevertheless, the capture of the reconnaissance schooner marked the inauspicious beginning of a particularly inept military effort by the French.

23 June

Byron weighed anchor on the morning of 23 June and set out for the head of the bay in search of the enemy, but the vagaries of the unfamiliar shallow channel soon compelled him to abandon the cumbersome *Fame*. Resuming his navigation in the *Fame*'s boats, he soon "saw sevl ships & vessls at anchor above them about 2 leag near a point of land (on the Northern shore) ... a frigate ... 2 others seemed to be Merchant or Storeships the others sloops and schooners in all 10 or 12 sail...."[3]

24 June

At dawn the next day Byron dispatched two boats to make further soundings, but within two hours they were compelled to return to the flagship with several French boats in pursuit.

On 24 June, Giraudais set his men to the rapid completion of the battery, being built en barbette, that he had begun on the north shore at Pointe à la Batterie. He transferred four 12-pounders and one 6-pounder from the *Machault*, his flagship, to the battery and appointed his second-in-command, Donat de la Garde,[4] to command the position. As a mobile supplement to the shore battery, Giraudais retained the *Machault* in readiness in the channel, close behind a chain of small sloops and schooners which he scuttled one-half cannon-shot below the battery.

The 60 men and seven women taken prisoner on their way to Quebec City in May, although "well used before the English ships appeared," were now packed into the hold of a small schooner for security reasons. According to the moving testimony of the prisoners, they were henceforth

without air, without light, strongly guarded by a party of soldiers, under the cannon of the battery; our cloaths and beds taken from us; we had not room to stretch ourselves ... [with] very little provisions and only brackish water to drink....[5]

25 June

On 25 June, the *Fame* weighed anchor and attempted to move closer to the head of the bay; however, at low water, at noon, it went aground [1]1 "on a patch of mud,"[6] "where I thought we never should have got off again."[7] It did get off, but only after nine or ten hours of arduous effort and jettisoning "one of her anchors for the present,"[8] and with the help of the schooner recaptured earlier off Miguasha Point.

It is difficult to comprehend Giraudais's failure to capitalize on the definite tactical advantage of having his adversary aground on the shoals. Decisive action by the French on 25 June might have altered the outcome of the encounter. However, the French commander was not altogether unmindful of his advantage. As Byron learned later, Giraudais has actually contemplated sending a boarding party to the *Fame*,[9] but had changed his mind when he perceived the man-of-war to be a fully armed two-decker.

The *Fame*'s admittedly formidable firepower notwithstanding, the French held enough of the classic advantages of a war situation to virtually guarantee their success: they enjoyed adequate manpower, the advantages of a secure defensive position, mobility both on land and on water, surprise, and for at least two hours before the *Fame* was released from the shoals, darkness. Their only serious disadvantage, albeit an essential one, was the low morale of both officers and men. Disheartened by the events both in Europe and North America in the previous two years which undermined France's position, neither Giraudais nor D'Angeac, any more than their subalterns, possessed the energy or bold offensive spirit which, combined with their physical advantages, might have led to a decisive French victory on the Restigouche in 1760.

26 June

On 26 June the rest of the English squadron came into view off Miguasha Point. While the captains of the ships of the line, the *Achilles* and the *Dorsetshire*, realized they were facing an unknown channel and prudently anchored east of the point, the captains of the frigates, the *Scarborough* and the *Repulse*, at first took the *Fame* to be French and endeavoured to get up to it. The enthusiasm of both Captain Scot and Captain Allen was exceeded only by their brash disregard of the navigational realities under which they were to labour. Both frigates ran aground and although the *Scarborough* was soon released thanks to assistance from the *Fame*, the *Repulse* was forced to spend the night on the shoals.[10]

27 June

His squadron at full complement now, on 27 June Byron ordered the *Fame*'s boats and the captured schooner to search for the elusive channel. The *Scarborough*, the *Repulse* and the *Fame* cautiously took up the rear.[11] The most serious disadvantage of the English, given the low morale of the French, was the hazardous navigation. The channel ran very close to the north shore and was therefore exposed to the French guns and musketry. It was also, as Byron put it, so narrow there was "no room for a ship to swing."[12]

28 June

When, on 28 June, the captured schooner went aground in less than a fathom,[13] it was clear that the English had unwittingly penetrated into a cul-de-sac. At the same time, the *Repulse* and the *Scarborough* lay aground within range of the French guns at Pointe à la Batterie. Giraudais gave the order to open fire, but the French action was limited to a rather passive and half-hearted effort and their fire caused little real damage to the English. Nevertheless, coupled with musketry from a detachment of regulars, Acadians and Mi'kmaq hidden in the surrounding woods, it harrassed the English in their efforts to get the ships afloat. However, the powerful artillery of the *Fame* was brought to bear on the French position as a cover for the grounded frigates and by evening the French musketry was effectively dispersed.

Giraudais reverted to the defensive once again, ordering the *Marquis de Malauze* and the *Bienfaisant* as far upstream in the Restigouche as

A	The *Fame*...	M.N.& O.	The *Repulse, Scarborough, & Schooner*...
B	The first Channel...		
C	The Second Channel, or So. Channel...	P.P.P.P.	The *Bienfaisant, Marquis de Malauze,* and all the Small Craft which were destroy'd.
D	The No. Channel...		
E	The No. Battery...		
F	Five Schooners & Sloops sunk...to prevent our passage.	Q	The Camp consisting of 1000 Regulars, Canadians and Savages.
G	The Enemys first Camp...		
HH	Sloops sunk in the narrows.	R	A Church and a Priest's House on So. point.
I	The hidden battery...		
K	The upper No. Battery en barbette...	S	The bay, only useful for flatboats
L	The *Machault*...		

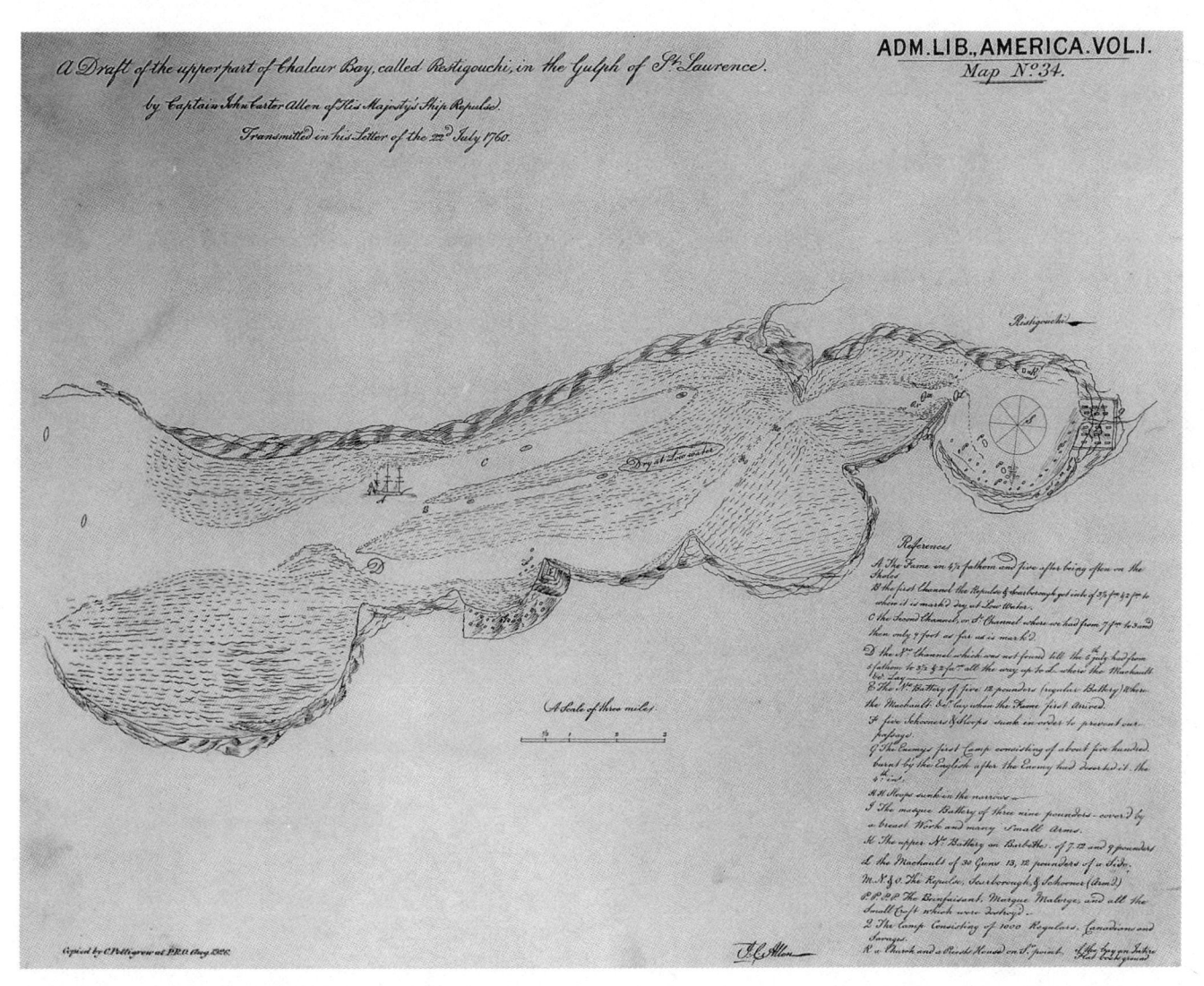

3 "A Draft of the upper part of Chaleur Bay, called Restigouchi, in the Gulph of St. Lawrence, by Captain John Carter Allen, of His Majesty's Ship *Repulse*. TO Scale of three miles." *(National Archives of Canada)*

possible in order to protect their cargoes.[14] He brought the *Machault* to the mouth of the river only slightly beyond the range of the English guns, later explaining: "I had considered remaining with my frigate to support the battery, but the strength of the enemy, being too great, would have prevented me from rejoining all the vessels that I had ordered upstream."[15]

As a further precaution, Giraudais ordered the English prisoners transferred from their prison aboard a schooner to the more secure hold of the *Machault* where they apparently underwent more severe treatment than previously.

The sailors were put into irons, and the captains and merchants had an old sail to lie on, spread on a row of hogsheads. Our allowance was bread and wine, with two ounces of pork per day; but, thank God, our appetites were not very keen; and if we complained that we were stifled with stench and heat, and eat up with vermin, they silenced us with saying, "Well, you shall go on shore under a guard of Indians," after telling us the savages had sworn they would scalp us every soul; they told us also, that, if we made the least noise, they would point four cannon into the hold and sink the vessel, of burn us like a parcel of rats.[16]

The search for a navigable channel remained Byron's essential first objective. He might well have dispensed with this exercise given the inability of the French to undertake a spirited defensive effort. Indeed, had he been willing to depart from the classical norm, Byron could well have landed a party, routed the French on shore, and then proceeded to harass the enemy squadron unimpeded.

The fact that even Byron's captured schooner, of low draft, had run aground while the *Machault* had retreated up river with relative ease was sufficient indication that considerable further effort was required before a passage could be found. Thus the soundings continued and during the night of 28-29 June a new and apparently promising channel was discovered close to the south shore of the Restigouche.

29 June

Byron immediately ordered the *Repulse* and the *Scarborough* to swing back and attempt the new passage, but further sounding soon belied his premature optimism. The passage, the "So[uth] channel" of the Allen map (or, more accurately, "the false South channel" as Giraudais called it[17]), was not

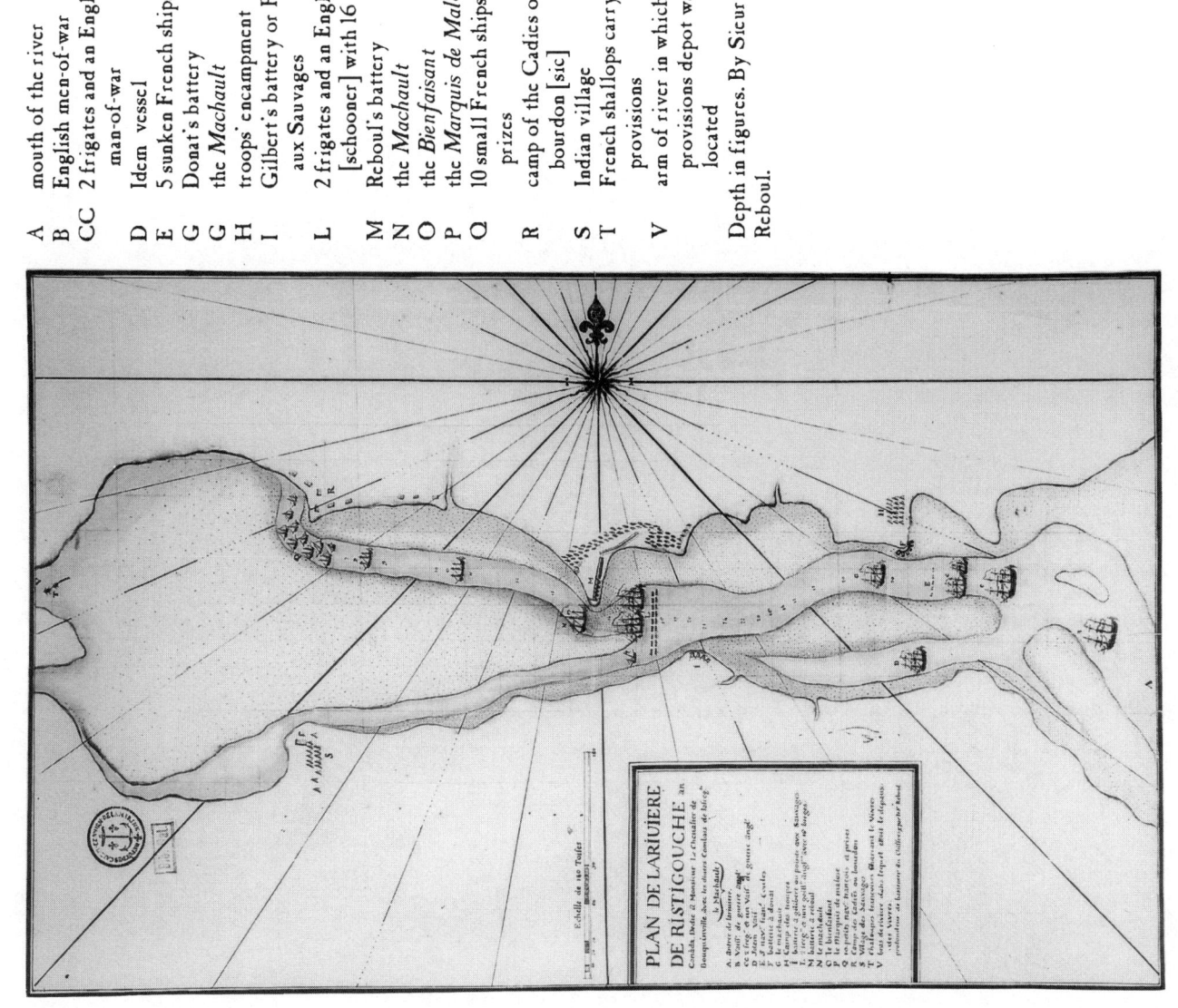

A   mouth of the river
B   English men-of-war
CC 2 frigates and an English man-of-war
D   Idem vessel
E   5 sunken French ships
G   Donat's battery
G   the *Machault*
H   troops' encampment
I   Gilbert's battery or Pointe aux Sauvages
L   2 frigates and an English [schooner] with 16 barges
M   Reboul's battery
N   the *Machault*
O   the *Bienfaisant*
P   the *Marquis de Malose* [sic]
Q   10 small French ships and prizes
R   camp of the Cadies or bourdon [sic]
S   Indian village
T   French shallops carrying provisions
V   arm of river in which the provisions depot was located

Depth in figures. By Sieur Reboul.

4 "Plan of the Ristigouche River in Canada. Dedicated to Monsieur le Chevalier de Bouquinville. With the various battles of the frigate *Machault*. Scale of 180 toises."*(Bibliothèque Nationale Ministère de la Défense [Marine], from a copy in the National Archives of Canada)*

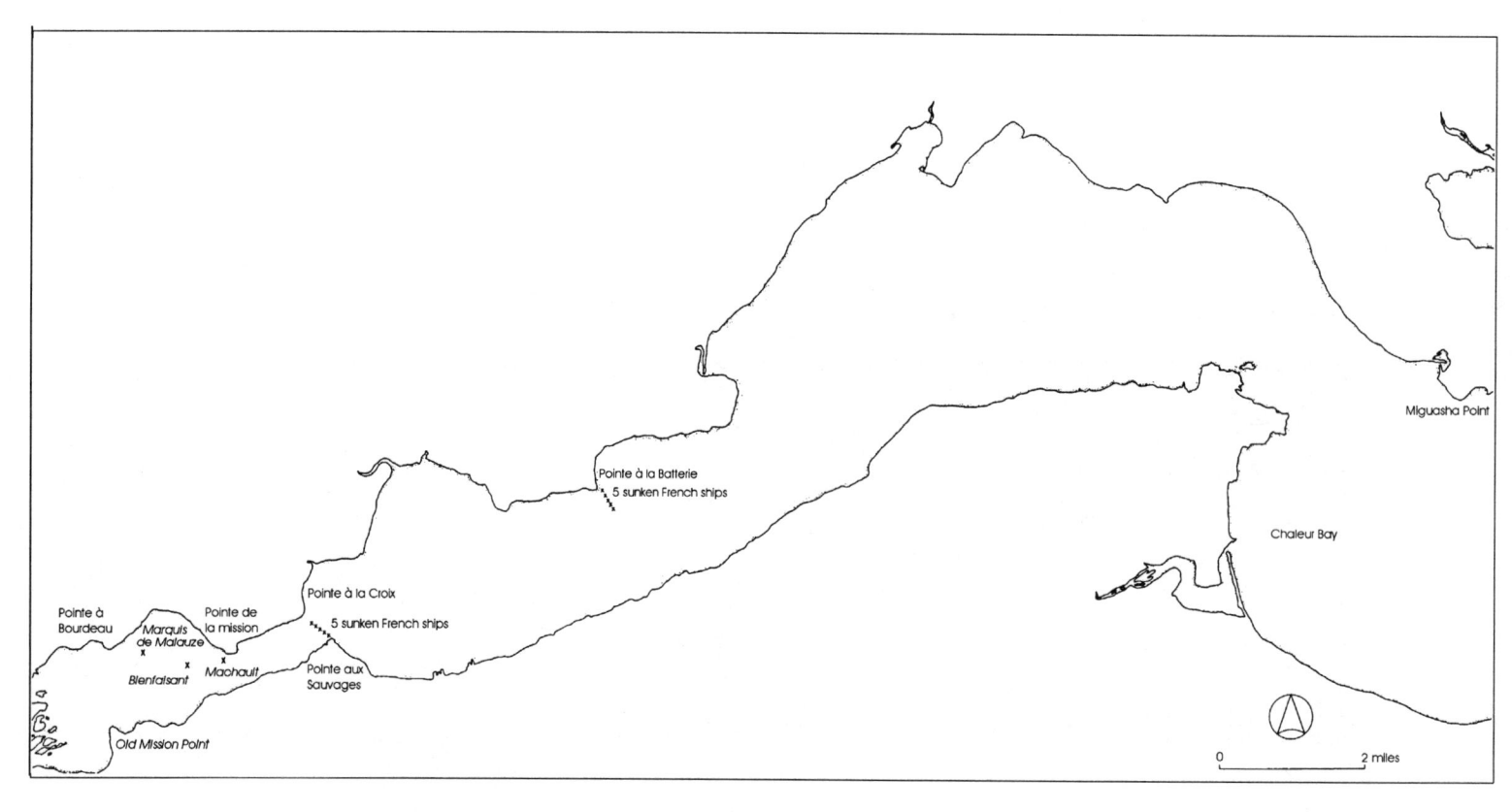

5 Restigouche River, showing the location of land and water sites. *(Map: S. Epps)*

a channel at all, but another cul-de-sac which from an impressive seven fathoms had quickly fallen to nine feet before running into mud flats at low water.

With the transfer of English efforts to the south channel on 29 June, the *Repulse* and the *Scarborough* fell beyond the range of the French guns at Pointe à la Batterie;[18] however, the battery remained within range of the powerful guns of the *Fame* which enjoyed the further and more significant advantage of firing at the unprotected French flank.[19] Although the French at first returned the *Fame*'s fire, they were overwhelmed within a few days.

2 July

By noon on 2 July, the *Fame* had smashed the easternmost French gun and a short time later the French began "making off from thence."[20] Their retreat was premeditated and orderly for the remaining four guns were spiked, "split and burst to pieces."[21]

When the English landing party put ashore at Pointe à la Batterie, not a Frenchman remained in sight. The gun carriages and other woodwork at both the battery and the adjoining camp were burned and the English, carrying their fury still further, also burned between 150 and 200 buildings which the Acadian refugee community had recently built.[22] This spirited action was the first decisive factor to affect English fortunes. Nevertheless, Byron declined his newly acquired land bridgehead, opting rather to maintain his original aim of finding a navigable channel and effecting the essential task of destroying the French squadron.

Following their withdrawal from Pointe à la Batterie on 2 July, the French reassembled at Pointe à Bourdeau where Giraudais ordered the establishment of a new camp and the unloading of his storeships. In an effort to stop the English advance, he ordered two new batteries erected at the mouth of the river, one on Pointe aux Sauvages (now within Campbellton) and the other across the narrows at Pointe de la Mission.

3 July

The day after the reduction of Pointe à la Batterie, Captain Allen of the *Repulse* dejectedly withdrew from the south channel. As he and Byron were discussing alternatives aboard the *Fame* on the evening of 3 July, "giving up all hopes of finding a channel."[23] word came that a new passage had been found close to the north shore where soundings had resumed the night prior to the French withdrawal from Pointe à la Batterie.

Heartened by this breakthrough, Byron ordered the *Repulse*, the *Scarborough* and the schooner (now armed with four 6-pounders and manned by 50 men) to prepare to move into the new channel. During the night of 3-4 July the English squadron began moving toward the river mouth, but it was two days before a passage could be cleared through the chain of hulks the French had sunk below Pointe à la Batterie.[24]

5 July

As soon as the English had cleared the chain of hulks below Pointe à la Batterie, on 5 July, Byron ordered the armed schooner against workmen he saw at the site of the new battery at Pointe aux Sauvages "to annoy them all he could with his great guns."[25] However, Lieutenant Cummings, the commander of the schooner, anchored too close to the shore, well within range of the deadly musketry which suddenly began to rain from the barely completed breastwork and the surrounding woods and was forced to draw back to safety. Cummings himself was seriously wounded, barely escaping with his life.[26]

6 to 7 July

Maintaining his original aim of protecting his cargos, during the night of 6-7 July Giraudais sank a second chain of five hulks across the channel at the narrows between Pointe aux Sauvages and Pointe à la Croix.[27] The English remained undaunted and showed every sign of continuing hard after the French. Giraudais then decided to transfer his prisoners from the *Machault* to the hold of the *Marquis de Malauze*, less vulnerable to immediate fire from the attackers. D'Angeac noted the transfer in his report: "We got rid of the prisoners we had aboard the *Machault* by putting them aboard the Marquis de Maloze [sic] with a detachment of twenty-five men and a sergeant and a Sergent de Confiance [sic] to guard them."[28]

When the English schooner again attempted to reduce the Pointe aux Sauvages battery on 7 July not only did it have concealed sniper musketry to contend with as before, but also the fire of three 4-pounders which now stood at the ready. In the face of superior firepower, a better position and a spirited French defence, the English again suffered the indignity of a hasty retreat to the safety of the frigates.[29]

Across the narrows at Pointe de la Mission another party of labourers had been busy erecting a second battery, en barbette, with an ordnance of three 12-pounders and two 6-pounders and a supporting detachment of 30 sharpshooters. This battery was ready to fire in the afternoon of 7 July.[30]

In the course of the night of 7–8 July, the *Repulse* and the *Scarborough*, preceded by the schooner, continued their advance and their survey of the channel. Although it is not clear how the English managed to skirt the second chain of hulks, they did so during the night of 7–8 July. Despite intermittent fire all night from both batteries and the musketry, at daybreak the schooner, the *Repulse* and the *Scarborough* all stood in the Restigouche, upstream from the French chain of hulks and face to face with the *Machault*.

8 July

As dawn broke on 8 July, Giraudais saw with dismay from the bridge of the *Machault* that the two English frigates and the armed schooner stood at anchor only one-half cannon-shot downstream. The engagement which the French had ardently hoped to avoid was inevitable and imminent. To the 32 guns of the *Repulse*, the 20 of the *Scarborough* and the four of the schooner were opposed the ten starboard 12-pounders of the *Machault*,[31] the three 4-pounders at Pointe aux Sauvages and the five guns at Pointe de la Mission. Every man who could be spared from manning the French artillery, guarding the prisoners in the *Marquis de Malauze*, and other tasks essential to the immediate defence of the French position was dispatched to disembark cargo from the two storeships and to tow a score or more smaller vessels within range of the French sharpshooters lining the north shore of the river.[32]

Shortly after five o'clock in the morning, the *Repulse*, now within range of the French battery on Pointe aux Sauvages, quickly drove the defenders from their position. As the frigates moved slowly upstream they were met by brisk fire from the battery on Pointe de la Mission and, close by, from the *Machault*.[33] The French fire was so brisk that the *Repulse*, in the lead, was driven "aground in a very bad position with her head on to the shoals."[34] The French fire inflicted such heavy punishment upon the *Repulse* that Giraudais claimed that technically his guns had sunk it.[35] Indeed, it is difficult to imagine how the *Repulse*, had it been standing in deep water rather than aground on the shoals, could have avoided sinking.

Far from being able to capitalize on the enemy's discomfort, the *Machault*, in an incredible example of military unpreparedness, was almost out of powder and cartridges.[36] As a safety precaution Giraudais had earlier transferred part of his war stores to a smaller vessel and to this vessel he hastily dispatched one of his boats. However, the terror of the moment affected its crew for they were never heard from again although the boat, fully laden as ordered, was later found abandoned.

As its powder supply dwindled the *Machault's* fire became more sporadic until it ceased at nine o'clock. The powder situation being compounded by the presence of seven feet of water in the hold, Giraudais determined to abandon ship[37] and at 11 o'clock the *Machault* struck its colours.

In the meantime the *Repulse* had managed to get off the shoals, and, with the *Scarborough*, resumed firing on the French battery at Pointe de la Mission. The latter's fire had virtually stopped when the *Machault* had struck its colours, but resumed at intervals, "not more than one or two guns in a quarter of an hour."[38] The English frigates were unable to move higher because of the shallow water.

Under ordinary circumstances, the tactic of storming the moribund *Machault* would have suited the occasion; however, Captain Allen of the *Repulse* surmised that the French intended to blow it up rather than turn its cargo over to the enemy. Given his irreversible advantage at this juncture, Allen accordingly held back his boats in order not to run unnecessary risk.[39]

Shortly before noon, Giraudais and D'Angeac, their determination to remain to the last aboard their flagship honoured now, descended into a boat and made for the French camp at Pointe à Bourdeau. Their orderly retreat did not even lack an appropriate flourish of enemy fire, "having, during part of the way, cannon shot hot on our heels."[40]

At or around noon the *Machault* blew up with a "very great explosion."[41] Presumably the charge had gone off prematurely for several Frenchmen were wounded. Fifteen minutes later the *Bienfaisant* similarly blew up, its entire cargo still in its hold.[42] The *Marquis de Malauze* would undoubtedly have suffered a similar fate had the prisoners not been within its hold. The prisoners, now numbering 62,[43] had heard the "two terrible reports." Shortly after, they were brought up on deck and ordered into an inadequate makeshift raft "which would have sunk with one half of our number." Half-crazed by the prospect of delivering themselves into the hands of the Mi'kmaq on shore, the prisoners refused to move and finally prevailed upon their captors to admit that to force them to leave would amount to sacrificing them to the Indians. The French therefore left them to their fate, but not before marching them back into the hold where they were fettered and handcuffed anew and the hatches again secured above them.[44]

The prisoners were "almost mad with fear, expecting every moment to be blown up," helpless in their dark and stifling prison. When a bulkhead was finally knocked down and the hatches forced open, what greeted them on deck was hardly more reassuring: dense smoke from the burning *Machault* and *Bienfaisant* stood between them and recognition by their compatriots beyond and "all the shore was lined with Indians, firing small arms upon us." Although fortunately out of musket range for the time being, they were in terror of night. "We were in the utmost perplexity to get away, because we knew, had we remained aboard that night, we should have been boarded by the Indians, and every man scalped."[45]

Ironically, the prisoners were responsible for the single most valiant feat of the entire Restigouche incident. A young fellow among them "who could swim very well" offered to set off for the *Repulse*, a full league downstream. Passing under the guns of the Pointe de la Mission battery, he arrived safely at the English frigate. Captain Allen immediately dispatched Lord Rutherford with nine boats escorted by the schooner to the *Marquis de Malauze* to the relief of the prisoners. Notwithstanding brisk fire from the one remaining French position, the English prisoners were all released and brought to the *Repulse* by mid-afternoon on 8 July.[46]

The English, determined to destroy every French vessel within their reach, set the *Marquis de Malauze* ablaze as soon as it was cleared of the prisoners. Like the *Bienfaisant*, its cargo of "wine and brandy, bales of goods and warlike stores" was jettisoned entirely. The efficiency of this aspect of the English operation was marred only by the death of six Englishmen, including a midshipman who, in spite of repeated calls to, had tarried too long with the liquor and went down with the flaming hulk.[47]

Rutherford's men continued their destruction of all available French shipping and by nightfall French losses totalled 22 or 23 vessels which, with the exception of the *Machault*, the *Bienfaisant* and the *Marquis de Malauze*, were mainly Acadian sloops, schooners and small privateers. (These figures do not include the ten vessels the French scuttled in the channel.) Like the *Machault* and the *Bienfaisant*, many had been set on fire by the French in order to avoid their falling into the hands of the enemy. One English source claims that of all the vessels in French hands on the morning of 8 July, only one schooner and two shallops remained by nightfall.[48]

Having thus burned and destroyed or caused to be destroyed everything within their reach in complete fulfillment of the aim of the expedition's singleminded commander, the *Repulse*, the *Scarborough* and the armed schooner swung around at 11 o'clock on the evening of 8 July and withdrew downstream. The French fleet destroyed, Byron did not even silence the empty tauntings of the one remaining enemy position, the Pointe de la Mission battery. After pausing off Pointe à la Batterie while rum was issued, Byron's squadron sailed. On 14 July, near Paspébiac, they met Wallis's squadron from Quebec City which had been searching the lower St. Lawrence and the gulf for the French ships, then continued on their way, four to the Fortress of Louisbourg and the *Repulse* to Halifax, "her rigging, masts and hull much shattered and no stores left at Louisbourg."[49]

After the unexpected and overwhelming attack of the British, the French were left to salvage what they could of the situation. Most of their ships' cargoes had been lost, many men had been killed,[50] and only a few boats were left to cross a large ocean. When St. Simon returned with Vaudreuil's instructions, the French had little means with which to implement them.

Sequels to the Battle

Undeterred by the bleak circumstances in which they now found themselves, the French fitted out some ships and plundered the trade in the area, captured several more prizes and even managed to send safely to France at least two ships, one under Giraudais which arrived in Santander on 27 October and the *Petit Marquis de Malauze* which reached St-Jean-de-Luz on 19 December 1760. The whole company of troops might have escaped had biscuit for the voyage been prepared in advance. The delay occasioned while provisions were prepared led to their entrapment by a second British expedition.[1]

The Capitulation Expedition

As early as the beginning of August British officials expressed the fear that the large number of French troops at Chaleur Bay would threaten British trade and communications. However, once Montréal capitulated in September the British were presented with an alternative to another attack. General Amherst wrote that Vaudreuil "had information [that the troops at Restigouche] were returned to France, but on my communicating to him the report [to the contrary], I now received, he sent an officer to the Bay des Chaleurs, with orders for the troops to lay down their arms according to the capitulation."[2] The officer representing French authority was Monsieur de Catalogne. Although Amherst felt that "M. de Vaudreuil would have done better to send an officer of higher rank,"[3] the British assented. Vaudreuil's orders were issued on 15 September and the ships sailed from Quebec City on 23 September 1760.[4] The men sent included Catalogne and "a field officer two Captains, four Subalterns, and one hundred and fifty men [under Major Elliott] from Quebec."[5] The *Repulse* and *Racehorse* were accompanied by the *Good Intent* transport and some schooners: a sufficient force to meet a depleted and discouraged group of soldiers now in alien territory.

In his report to the Admiralty, Captain Macartney of the *Racehorse* gave a full account of the fleet's activities. After anchoring in the Restigouche on 23 October 1760, they met with the Indians and the troops. On 29 October the French decided to surrender quietly, embarked on the *Good Intent* and departed for France on 5 November. In an appended note, Macartney gave a succinct account of the state of the post and the changes which his visit brought:

Peace being concluded with the Mickmack Indians and the Scalping Knife and Tomahawk buryed in token and security thereof, one hundred and ninety six Regulars under the Command of Monsr Don Jacque Captain, with Eighty Seamen Capt. Gramont Comm^r yielded themselves up prisoners according to the articles of Capitulation, and were put on board Good Intent Transport to be conveyed to France, agreeable to the notification in my orders.

The Number of Inhabitants at Restigouche amounts to one thousand and three, including men women and children.

The Number of Indians we could get no just account of but appears to consist of 3 or 400.

We spiked up and destroyed two batterys of Canon, one of 4-12 prs and 1-6 pr, and the other of 3 small

6 "On the River Restigouche, looking down towards the Peak of Campbellton." *(Canadian Illustrated News, 19 August 1882, p. 120)*

7 "Looking up the Restigouche from La Petite Rochelle [near Pointe à Bourdeau]." *(Canadian Illustrated News, 19 August 1882, p. 120)*

pieces, which the Enemy had erected on two points upon the side of the Bason in order to hinder our ships from getting up. We found besides at Restigouche 1-18 pr, 1-9 pr, and 1-6 pr which was also spiked up.
We found and brought away in the Schooners 320 barrels of Powder, some shoes and cloathing.
We burnt one Schooner repairing, and one sloop, and sold a small schooner to the French.
We brought away The Polly Sloop (from Boston loaded with Rum) which had been taken by the French. The Resolution (from Piscaluway with Molasses and sugar) also taken. And a Small Sloop that was a Privateer belonging to Monsʳ Ablong at Ristigouche. English Prisoners, 12 Men, 7 Women and 4 children which we also brought away.[6]

Major Elliott reported:

We were employed till the 5th Novʳ in getting on board the Stores from their Magazines, in which was 327 barrels powder, Muskett ball, small shot, Blankets, Coarse Brown Cloth, Flour, Pork, Wine, Rum, Brandy ... the Powder was all brought away, the Shot I threw into the River, where it was impossible for them to get them out; the rest of the Goods I desired the Capts. of Militia to divide equally amongst the Inhabitants.[7]

The men had carried out their orders with dispatch and efficiency.

The little British fleet had more trouble in leaving than in coming for a severe storm arose immediately after their passage through Canso Narrow and the ships were scattered. The *Good Intent* reached France with little mishap, as reported by the French clerk Bazagier,[8] but the *Swan*, on which Major Elliott was sailing, struck on Sable Island. The passengers and crew reached shore, but all the equipment and supplies were lost. The *Racehorse* had to steer for England. Two ships under Captain Carter and Lieutenant Shaw arrived in New York, and Captain Allen took the *Repulse* to Halifax.

Visitors to Restigouche in 1761

The Restigouche area was not deserted after the capitulation expedition. Indians and Acadians still populated the area and petitioned the British for attention. Most of the French soldiers had been deported in the fall of 1760, but a small picket of 12 men under Niverville had been sent to Miramichi before this occurred and had never surrendered.[9] Nor was the area completely isolated; several administrative or commercial expeditions went there in 1761 before the British carried out the final sequel to the battle of the Restigouche.

The first to visit in the spring of 1761 was a man named Grandmaison, under orders to seize a deserter from the 35th Regiment named Guillaume Cart. He arrived on 20 March with six unarmed men. When wounded by Cart while trying to execute his orders, Grandmaison returned to Quebec City after sending couriers to Niverville to inform him of the capitulation.[10]

In mid-July, Pierre du Calvet set out for Chaleur Bay in a large sloop, *Ste-Anne*, commanded by Captain Joanis with an eight-man crew. His mission was to take a census of the Acadians in the area for the Quebec government. This he carried out all along Restigouche River and Chaleur Bay for by this time many Acadians had left Old Mission Point and Pointe à Bourdeau and moved to sites along Chaleur Bay. Du Calvet returned to Quebec City in October 1761.[11]

A third non-destructive expedition also sailed from Quebec City. Gamaliel Smethurst, in a trading vessel fitted out in Marblehead, Massachusetts, went to trade with the French and Indians in the summer of 1761. But just as Smethurst was about to sail from Nepisiguit (Bathurst) in late October, his vessel loaded with about 120 tons of dry fish and oil, he encountered the expedition ordered to destroy the post on the Restigouche.[12] This ruined further trade and, to make matters worse, Smethurst abandoned by his vessel and was forced to make his way along the coast to Fort Cumberland.

Fearing that the continuation of the Restigouche post constituted a threat to British trade and communications, the British had decided to clear the area. Captain Roderick Mackenzie, of Fort Cumberland, led the expedition to remove the Acadian inhabitants. A newspaper account relates the incident:

We hear from Nova Scotia, That sometime last Month Capt. Mackenzie of Fort Cumberland, having armed two Vessels at Bay Vert, proceeded as far to the Northward as the Bay Challeurs, in order to break up a nest of French Vermin on that Coast, who have done so much Mischief these two or three Years past, in intercepting our Vessels bound to Halifax, Louisbourgh, and the River St. Lawrence, which he happily effected; And having taken about 240 Men, Women and Children Prisoners, brought them to Bay Vert; together with 8 or 10 small Vessels loaded with their effects. All the other small Craft upon the Coast be destroyed, so that there need be no Apprehension of any Interruption in going up the

River next year, as all the Ringleaders of the Mischief hitherto done with their families, are now Prisoners.[13]

The 1765 census, showing only 145 men, women and children, indicates Mackenzie's thoroughness.[14]

Conclusion

The battle of the Restigouche can be viewed in two contexts: as one episode in the history of naval engagements and as one factor affecting the political history of Canada.

In terms of battle itself, its most striking aspect was the almost slavish adherence of Captain Byron to the rules of naval action. A more imaginative and bolder commander (perhaps John Carter Allen) might have achieved the destruction of the French fleet with equal efficiency and greater speed: landing a party of marines at the time the antagonists came into contact would have achieved Byron's aim in short order. Certainly the superiority of English firepower warranted a departure from the classic steps, especially if the British realized that the state of French morale prevented Giraudais from capitalizing on his tactical advantages.

Giraudais's primary aim was to save, at all costs, the fleet entrusted to him for the relief of New France. To this end his was initially the most advantageous situation: the French enjoyed superior manpower, a secure defensive position, mobility on both land and water, and surprise. The one essential disadvantage of the French was low morale. Events both in Europe and North America had undermined the morale of officers and men alike and neither Giraudais nor D'Angeac possessed the energy and bold offensive spirit that would have allowed the French to seize the advantage of their favourable strategical and tactical situation on the Restigouche River in June and July of 1760.

The battle is notable, too, as the last naval engagement between Great Britain and France for the possession of North America.

In terms of the political history of Canada, the battle played a significant part in determining the future of New France. Even though the assistance sent them was not what officials in Montréal had hoped for — the fleet carried fewer men and supplies than had been requested, it sailed from France much later than planned, and only three of the six ships reached New France — subsequent events might have been altered if they could have made use of what men and supplies did reach New France. Without the men and supplies, the attempt to regain Quebec City from the British had to be abandoned. Montréal was less able to resist British attack, and the basis of a strong French position in Acadia was lost before it could be established. At length Montréal capitulated and New France became British. The fall of New France may not have been a necessary result of the battle of the Restigouche, but the loss of the fleet did precipitate it.

Notes

Introduction

1. John Knox, *An Historical Journal of the Campaigns in North America*, ed. A. G. Doughty (Toronto: The Champlain Society, 1916), Vol. 3, pp. 353-421.

Background to the Fleet's Departure for New France

1. Francois Gaston, duc de Lévis, *Collection des manuscrits du maréchal de Lévis*, ed. H. R. Casgrain (Montréal: Beauchemin et fils, 1890), pp. 262-3. [Note: All quotes from French references have been translated.]
2. Canada. National Archives (hereafter cited as NA), MG1, $C^{11}A$, Vol. 104, Vaudreuil to minister, 9 Nov. 1759, p. 126.
3. NA, MG1, $C^{11}A$, Vol. 104, Lévis to minister, 11 Nov. 1759, p. 123.
4. Francois Gaston, duc de Lévis, op. cit., pp. 263-5.
5. NA, MG2, B^1, Vol. 66, Projet des forces à employer contre les Anglais en 1760 et des mesures à prendre à ce sujet, 28 Nov. 1760, fol. 243.
6. NA, MG1, $C^{11}A$, Vol. 105, Part 2, Le Mercier to minister, 7 Jan. 1760, pp. 488-96.
7. NA, MG1, B, Vol. 110, president of Navy Board to Gradis, 10 Dec. 1759, pp. 380-3.
8. Cf. Berryer to Rostan, 2 May and 28 Nov. 1760 in Jean de Maupassant, *Les deux expéditions de Pierre Desclaux* (Bordeaux: Feret, 1915), p. 26.

The Voyage from Bordeaux to Canada

1. NA, MG2, B^4, Vol. 98, Journal de la Campagne du S. Giraudais Sur le N^{re} le *Machault*, by Giraudais, Oct. 1760, p. 6.
2. NA, MG1, B, Vol. 112, Part 1, president of Navy Board to Rostan, 9 May 1760, fol. 193.
3. NA, MG1, B, Vol. 112, Part 1, Instructions sur la Campagne que le Sr de la Giraudais va faire en Canada, 15 Feb. 1760, fol. 104.
4. *New York Mercury*, 28 July 1760.
5. NA, MG1, $C^{11}A$, Vol. 105, Part 2, Fiedmond to minister, 18 May 1760, p. 596.
6. NA, MG12, WO34, Vol. 11, Campbell to Lawrence, 22 July 1760, p. 57.
7. *New York Mercury*, 1 Sept. 1760.
8. Ibid.
9. *Boston Newsletter*, 31 July 1760.
10. *Annual Register for 1760* (London: J. Dodsley, 1781), pp. 134-7.

Chaleur Bay

1. NA, MG1, B, Vol. 112, Part 1, Instructions sur la Campagne que le Sr de la Giraudais va faire en Canada, 15 Feb. 1760, fol. 104.
2. NA, MG1, F^3, Vol. 50, 14 Aug. 1758.
3. NA, MG1, $C^{11}A$, Vol. 105, Part 1, Vaudreuil to minister, 17 Aug. 1760, pp. 307 ff.
4. George Macbeath, "The Struggle for Acadia," *Collections of the New Brunswick Historical Society*, No. 15 (1915), p. 41.
5. The post's establishment is usually dated at 1758 in secondary sources, but Pierre du Calvet states that only in May 1759 were the King's Magazines moved to Restigouche (*The Case of Peter du Calvet* [London: n.p., 1784], p. 3).
6. Antoine Bernard, *Histoire de la survivance acadienne* (Montréal: Les Clercs de Saint-Viateur [1935]), p. 28.
7. NA, MG2, B^4, Vol. 98, Relations depuis Notre depart de Royant jusqu'au Jour de Notre Combat avec les Anglais Le huit Juillet mil Sept cent Soixante, by D'Angeac, 5 Aug. 1760.

Reactions to the Fleet's Arrival

1. George McKinnon Wrong, *The Fall of Canada* (Oxford: Clarendon Press, 1974), p. 186.
2. NA, *Report for the Year 1905* (Ottawa: King's Printer, 1906), [hereafter cited as NAR], Vol. 1, p. 47.
3. Ibid., p. 48.
4. Comte de Malartic, *Journal des Campagnes au Canada de 1755 à 1760* (Paris: E. Plon, Nourrit, 1890), p. 335.
5. NAR, Vol. 1, pp. 46-7.
6. NA, MG2, B^f, Vol. 30, Evénements du Canada depuis Le Mois d'Octobre 1759 Jusqu'au mois de Septembre 1760, pp. 286-95.
7. NA, MG1, C^{II}A, Vol. 87, Part 3, Vaudreuil to D'Angeac, 17 June 1760, pp. 368-83.
8. NA, MG1, E, Carton 21, Bigot to minister, 20 June 1760, p. 4.
9. Comte de Malartic, op. cit., p. 335.
10. NA, MG18, L1, Colville Memoirs, pp. 46-7; NA, MG11, CO5, Vol. 58, Colville to Cleveland, 12 Sept. 1760, p. 593.
11. NAR, Vol. 1, p. 48.
12. NA, MG11, CO5, Vol. 59, Hill to Whitmore, 14 June 1760, p. 29.
13. NA, MG12, Adm. 1/1491, Byron to Admiralty, 11 July 1760; *Boston Newsletter*, 17 July 1760.

The Battle

1. NA, MG12, Adm. 51/3830, A journal of the Proceedings of HMS *Fame* [hereafter cited as *Fame* journal].
2. John Knox, op. cit., Vol. 3, p. 394.
3. *Fame* journal.
4. John Knox, op. cit., Vol. 3, p. 363.
5. *Annual Register for 1760*, op. cit., p. 136.
6. *Fame* journal.
7. NA, MG12, Adm. 1/482, Byron to Colville, 14 July 1760, p. 129.
8. *Fame* journal.
9. NA, MG12, Adm. 1/1491, Byron to Admiralty, 11 July 1760. Neither Giraudais nor D'Angeac mention this incident in their narratives.
10. *Fame* journal.
11. Ibid.
12. NA, MG12, Adm. 1/1491, Byron to Admiralty, 11 July 1760.
13. Ibid.
14. Ibid.
15. John Knox, op. cit., Vol. 3, p. 363.
16. *Annual Register for 1760*, op. cit., p. 136.
17. John Knox, op. cit., Vol. 3, p. 363.
18. Ibid.
19. The French battery was built en barbette, that is, with its guns firing over the parapet as opposed to firing through embrasures.
20. *Fame* journal. Giraudais's narrative implies 3 July, but from the other evidence, this is an error.
21. NA, MG12, Adm. 1/1491, Byron to Admiralty, 11 July 1760.
22. NA, MG12, Adm. 1/482, Byron to Colville, 14 July 1760, p. 129.
23. NA, MG12, Adm. 1/1491, Byron to Admiralty, 11 July 1760.
24. NA, MG12, Adm. 1/1442, Allen to Admiralty, 2 Aug. 1760.
25. NA, MG12, Adm. 1/1491, Byron to Admiralty, 11 July 1760.
26. Ibid.
27. The only evidence for the date of the second boom is the requisitioning of an Acadian vessel on 6 July (NA, RG4, A1, Vol. 1, 6 July 1760, p. 23).
28. John Knox, op. cit., Vol. 3, p. 370.
29. Ibid., p. 369.
30. Ibid.; *Fame* journal.

31 Giraudais deployed three as well on the port side "in case their barges should come during the battle and approach you from that side." (John Knox, op. cit., Vol. 3, p. 364).
32 Ibid.
33 *Fame* journal; NA, MG12, Adm. 1/1442, Allen to Admiralty, 2 Aug. 1760.
34 NA, MG12, Adm. 1/1491, Byron to Admiralty, 11 July 1760.
35 John Knox, op. cit., Vol. 3, p. 365.
36 Ibid., p. 370.
37 Ibid.
38 *Fame* journal.
39 NA, MG12, Adm. 1/1491, Byron to Admiralty, 11 July 1760.
40 John Knox, op. cit., Vol. 3, pp. 370-1.
41 *Fame* journal.
42 NA, MG12, Adm. 1/1491, Byron to Admiralty, 11 July 1760.
43 Ibid.; NA, MG12, Adm. 1/482, Byron to Colville, 14 July 1760, p. 129; *Fame* journal.
44 *Annual Register for 1760*, op. cit., p. 136.
45 Ibid.
46 Ibid.
47 NA, MG12, Adm. 1/1491, Byron to Admiralty, 11 July 1760.
48 Ibid.; *Fame* journal; John Knox, op. cit., Vol. 3, p. 365.
49 NA, MG12, Adm. 1/1491, Byron to Admiralty, 11 July 1760.
50 See NA, MG8, G26, Vols. 1 and 2, Sainte-Anne de Ristigouche, 1759-1795, Vol. 1, pp. 30-1, Vol. 2, pp. 28-30.

Sequels to the Battle

1 NA, MG1, C^{11}A, Vol. 105, Part 2, Observations sur certaines mouvemens en Nouvelle France, 1760, pp. 471-86.
2 NA, MG11, CO5, Vol. 59, Amherst to Pitt, 17 Sept. 1760, p. 125.
3 NA, MG21, G2, Vol. 1, Amherst to Haldimand, 15 Sept. 1760, pp. 130-1.
4 NA, MG11, CO5, Vol. 59, Part 2, Vaudreuil, 15 Sept. 1760, p. 43; NA, MG12, WO34, Vol. 1, Murray to Amherst, 24 Sept. 1760, pp. 6-7.
5 NA, MG12, Adm. 1/2112, Colville to Macartney, 18 Sept. 1760.
6 NA, MG12, Adm. 1/2112, Macartney to Admiralty, 11 Dec. 1760.
7 NA, MG11, CO5, Vol. 61, Part 2, Elliot to Amherst, 24 Jan. 1761, p. 24.
8 NA, MG1, C^{11}A, Vol. 105, Part 2, Bazagier to minister for Colonies, 4 Dec. 1760, p. 420.
9 NA, MG12, WO34, Vol. 1, Murray to Amherst, 22 Feb. 1761, p. 35.
10 NA, MG12, WO34, Vol. 1, Grandmaison to Murray, 26 March 1761, p. 69.
11 Ibid., pp. 301-31.
12 Gamaliel Smethurst, "Gamaliel Smethurst's Narrative of his Journey from Nepisiguit to Fort Cumberland in 1761," ed. W.F. Ganong, *Collection of the New Brunswick Historical Society*, No. 6 (1905), pp. 358-90.
13 *The Boston Newsletter*, 10 Dec. 1761.
14 Quebec (Province) Archives, *Rapport de l'archiviste de la province de Québec*, Vol. 17 (Quebec City: King's Printer, 1936-37), pp. 113-4.

References Cited

The Annual Register, or A View of the History, Politics, and Literature, for the year 1760.
J. Dodsley, London, 1781.

Bernard, Antoine
Histoire de la survivance acadienne, 1755-1935. Les Clercs de Saint-Viateur, Montréal, 1935.

Boston Newsletter
1760.

Canada. National Archives.
Report ... for the Year, 1905. King's Printer, Ottawa, 1906. 3 vols.

Canada. National Archives. Manuscript Division.
MG1, Series B (Lettres envoyées, 1663-1789)
MG1, C^{11}A (Correspondance générale, Canada, 1540-1785)
MG1, E (Dossiers personnels, 1638-1791)
MG1, F^3 (Collection Moreau de St-Méry, 1492-1798)
MG2, B^1 (Délibérations du Conseil de Marine, 1715-1786)
MG2, B^4 (Campagnes, 1640-1782)
MG8, G (Archives paroissiales, 1621-1929)
MG11, CO5 (America and West Indies, 1689-1819)
MG12, Adm. 1 (Secretary's Department, In-letters)
MG12, Adm. 51 (Captains' Logs)
MG12, WO34 (Amherst Papers)
MG18, L1 (Colville Memoirs)
MG21, G2 (Haldimand Papers)
RG4, A1 (S Series, 1760-1840)

Canadian Illustrated News
1882.

du Calvet, Pierre
The Case of Peter du Calvet, esq., of Montreal in the Province of Quebeck. N.p., London, 1784.

Knox, John
An Historical Journal of the Campaigns in North America for the Years 1757, 1758, 1759, and 1760. Editor, A.G. Doughty. The Champlain Society, Toronto, 1914-16. 3 vols.

Lévis, François Gaston, duc de
Collection des manuscrits du maréchal de Lévis. Editor, H.R. Casgrain. Beauchemin, Montréal, 1890. Vol. 2.

Macbeath, George
"The Struggle for Acadia" *Collections of the New Brunswick Historical Society,* No. 15 (1959), pp. 27-41. Saint John, N.B.

Malartic, [Anne Joseph Hippolyte] de Maurés, comte de
Journal des Campagnes au Canada de 1755 à 1760.... E. Plon, Nourrit, Paris, 1890.

Maupassant, Jean de
Les deux expéditions de Pierre Desclaux au Canada (1759 et 1760). Feret, Bordeaux, 1915.

New York Mercury
1760.

Quebec (Province) Archives.
Rapport de l'archiviste de la province de Québec. Vol. 17. King's Printer, Quebec City, 1936-37.

Smethurst, Gamaliel
"Gamaliel Smethurst's Narrative of his Journey from Nepisiguit to Fort Cumberland in 1761." Editor, W.F. Ganong. *Collections of the New Brunswick Historical Society,* No. 6 **(1905)**. pp. 358-90. Saint John, N.B.

Wrong, George McKinnon
The Fall of Canada, A Chapter in the History of the Seven Year's War.... The Clarendon Press, Oxford, 1914.